Where Is Here?

CANADIAN CULTURAL POLICY
IN A GLOBALIZED WORLD

Where Is Here?

CANADIAN CULTURAL POLICY
IN A GLOBALIZED WORLD

Joyce Zemans

THE JOHN P. ROBARTS PROFESSOR
OF CANADIAN STUDIES

TENTH ANNUAL ROBARTS LECTURE
Wednesday, March 13, 1996
York University, North York, Ontario

ROBARTS CENTRE FOR CANADIAN STUDIES

CANADIAN CATALOGUING IN PUBLICATION DATA

Zemans, Joyce, 1940-
Where is here? : Canadian cultural
policy in a globalized world

(Robarts lecture ; 10th)
Lecture presented at York University, Mar. 13, 1996.
Includes bibliographical references.
ISBN 1-55014-342-5

1. Canada – Cultural Policy.   1. Robarts Centre for
Canadian Studies. 11. Title. 111. Series: Robarts
Centre for Canadian Studies lecture series ; 10.

NX750.C3Z45 1997   700'.971   C97-932619-3

The artwork pictured on the cover is *Geometry*
by Judith Schwarz, 1989, steel bar and mahogany,
reproduced by permission of the artist.

Imaging by ECW *Type & Art*, Oakville, Ontario.
Printed by The Porcupine's Quill, Inc., Erin, Ontario.

Published by the Robarts Centre for Canadian Studies,
York University, North York, Ontario M3J 1P3.

CENTRE

ROBARTS
CENTRE

JOYCE ZEMANS is an art historian, curator and arts administrator whose research and teaching is focussed on Canadian art and cultural policy. Appointed University Professor in 1995, she is a former Dean of York's Faculty of Fine Arts (1985–88) and former Director of the Canada Council (1989–92). She has served on a number of Canadian and international policy fora including the Japan — U.S. Comparative Cultural Policy Project, UCLA (1993–1996); the Canada-Japan Forum 2000 (1992–94); The Institute for Research on Public Policy (1990–92); and the Commonwealth Arts Administrators expert working group on cultural relations (1990–91). Prof. Zemans is Co-Director of the MBA Programme in Arts and Media Administration in the Schulich School of Business at York University.

As the Robarts Chair in Canadian Studies at York (1995–96), she focussed her research on Canadian cultural policy, organizing the Robarts Seminars on "Cultural Sovereignty in a Globalized World: The Future of Cultural Policy in Canada."

FOREWORD

This paper analyzes the current policy environment for culture in Canada. In particular, it focuses on the need for a comprehensive strategy for Canadian culture that will take us in into the 21st century.

The paper is based, in part, on the Robarts seminars, held at York University in the fall of 1995, which identified some of the problems that face us and areas in which we must take action. To understand where we are going, we have also to understand where we have been. Despite my original, albeit naive, desire to lay out a Canadian cultural policy for the 21st century, I have, in this Robarts Lecture, restricted myself to broader strokes, reviewing past actions and their implications for the current environment. Through this analysis, I have attempted to establish the importance of a coherent policy in the cultural sector. The arts and cultural sector is key to understanding the changing roles of the citizen and the nation. It is central to education and preparation for life in the knowledge age; to job creation in a world in which traditional jobs are quickly disappearing, and to the way in which Canada will define itself in the 21st century.

It is widely believed that Canada's destiny, culturally and historically, finds its fulfillment in being a nation, and that nationality is essential to identity. It seems to me, on the other hand, quite clear that we are moving towards a post-national world and that Canada has moved further in that direction than any of the smaller nations. What is important about the last century, in this country, is not that we have been a nation for a hundred years but that we have had a hundred years to make the transition from a pre-national to a post-national consciousness.

— Northrop Frye, *The Modern Century*, 1967 (17)

The Current Environment:
Globalization and Neo-conservatism

Northrop Frye has defined Canada's national dilemma as the familiar existential search — with a significant twist. For Frye, the Canadian question was not "Who am I?" but "Where is here?" Today, however, the future of "here" is in question. In face of the twin spectres of globalization and technology, political scientists, economists and technocrats, like Frye before them, are predicting the end of the nation as we know it. Moreover, a new dimension has been added to the debate. If, historically, the cost of culture was at issue within the nation state, the new value system being imposed by neoconservative forces today challenges not only the borders of the state but also the power of the public sector, eroding notions of the public interest and a community of shared experiences, and challenging the state to cede responsibility to the marketplace.

It may, therefore, seem foolhardy and naive to propose to discuss a topic soon destined to become irrelevant. Yet while I appreciate the implications of this new world view, I remain convinced that we will be discussing variations on this theme fifty years from now; I believe, in fact, that the issue is likely to become more, rather than less, relevant in the new knowledge age in which economic and political objectives are more closely bound up with cultural objectives than ever before. As borders continue to become economically and culturally more porous, and boundaries between national and international activities continue to shift, Canada must replace rhetoric and piecemeal strategies with a long-term, comprehensive and integrated cultural policy.

Culture is not static and no culture, if it is to survive and grow, can be isolated from external or internal influence. As Northrop Frye has written, culture requires stimulation from outside as well as from within national borders (Frye 53). At the same time, Frye argues that all culture is essentially local, created out of the tension-filled relations between local forces and the centre and between the centre and external forces. We have then the perfect conditions for an exciting cultural environment. No one would suggest that Canada is short of tensions. Nor do we lack external stimulation.

We are, without question, one of the most open societies in the world. Canada on a per capita basis is the largest cultural-sector importer in the world.[1] We are a country dominated by American cultural product, in a world deemed "globalized" by technology and by a dominant value system of wealth and competition.[2] The FTA/NAFTA cultural exemption clause offers no solace. In fact, fear of retaliation under the "notwithstanding clause" has significantly restricted our capacity to act in well-defined areas of need in fields such as film distribution and, I would argue, in developing the comprehensive policy we require.[3]

Facing many of the challenges which confront Canada today, particularly in light of the prospect of a unified Europe, and recognizing the importance of an established framework for planning in the cultural field, in 1988 the Council of Europe embarked upon a comprehensive review of national cultural policies on a country-by-country basis. An examination of these policies makes it evident that in Europe, cultural policy has become a well-established field of inquiry. Clear purposes and objectives are directly tied to success in policy implementation.

Grappling with similar issues as it moves into the Asian sphere of influence, the Australian government issued its "Creative Nation Statement" in 1994. Like the European policy studies, the Australian document offers a model for Canada in its recognition of the need for setting out first principles and acknowledging the importance of federal leadership in cultural policy. Although the present government no longer seems bound by it, the statement defines government responsibilities for cultural development in five principal categories: nurturing creativity and excellence, enabling all to enjoy the widest range of cultural experience, preserving the nation's heritage, promoting the expression of Australia's cultural identity, and developing sustainable cultural industries. Citing the "Creative Nation" program and noting the contrast with Canada, Richard Gwyn wrote:

> ... just as Australians are ahead of us in understanding that their past speaks to their present, they are ahead of us in understanding the role of institutions in nurturing a sense of civitas. (288)

Canada should also have undertaken a comprehensive cultural policy review to obtain a realistic assessment of what we have accomplished and to determine the strategies that we will require to accommodate the changing environment. But unlike most European countries, Canada has not clearly formulated its purpose in the creation of cultural policy. The 1951 Massey-Levesque Report is as close as we have come in this regard. Without the clarity of purpose which underlies policy development in many European countries or an understanding of what has been achieved, we have no framework for action. Thus a multitude of government task forces and parliamentary committee reports on various aspects of Canadian culture continue to accumulate dust on Ottawa shelves, and governments remain incapable of coherent forward planning or developing appropriate responses to external forces. Despite the urgent need for a comprehensive vision encompassing technology and content and policy as well as market-driven strategies, responsibility for communications has been even further isolated from the cultural portfolio since its transfer from Canadian Heritage to the Department of Industry. And although the government announced in 1994 that culture represents the third pillar of Canadian foreign policy, alongside diplomacy and trade, Radio Canada International almost disappeared in April 1996 with no department prepared to take responsibility for its future.[4]

In developing policy, it is critical to understand fully the factors that consciously or unconsciously are brought to bear on its creation. John Meisel calls on Harold Innis' image of history as a "web of which the warp and the woof are space and time woven in a very uneven fashion and producing distorted patterns" to analyze the extrinsic and intrinsic factors in both time and space which influence the creation of cultural policy (49). First then a brief analysis of what has changed in the warp and the woof.

In its 1951 report, the Massey-Levesque Commission questioned the purpose of elaborate national defense strategies if, as a nation, we were not clear about what we were defending.⁵ With the Cold War over and the vision of a peace dividend in sight, Ursula Franklin warns that today the social institution of war has been transmuted and updated with a "set of modern instruments to assist in the struggle for global hegemony." Economic competition and conflict have taken on the characteristics of active warfare:

> The new battlefields are in those territories . . . that are the home of the common good, of art, of friendship and scholarship, of whatever is held in common and cannot be cut up into private parcels of property. (15)

Whatever cannot be bought and sold or expressed in terms of financial transactions stands in the way of the market and is enemy territory to be occupied, transformed and conquered.

Franklin is one of the strongest of the new social critics with her evocation of a technological transposition where the territory of non-market forces and its inhabitants have become the new enemy. In this world, as the machine becomes more powerful, people and the things they value are declared worthless:

> . . . we are in the middle of a market-driven war on the common good. People are valued as buyers and sellers, or as customers or clients and there is no recognition that their values, their vitality and their sustenance comes out of a collectivity of interests, a community of shared experiences. (15)

Franklin would have agreement from John Ralston Saul who argued vehemently in the 1995 Massey Lectures for the importance of the public space, describing the key elements of contemporary Canadian society (which are inexorably reducing that space) as the market place, technology, globalization, and the money markets (*Unconscious Civilization* 134).

What Franklin, Saul and numerous other eloquent voices that have arisen in the last several years are describing is the rapid delegitimization of the public sphere. This paradigm shift has had serious implications for the arts and culture. Evidence of this shift lies in the transformation in the focus of Canadian cultural policy away from a nationalist, public service, market corrective approach towards a growing emphasis on a market ideology. (Theodor Adorno suggests that in this new environment, policy is designed primarily to eliminate obstacles to the commoditization of culture and to support the cultural industries.) Despite the peace dividend, the March 1996 federal budget's four year proposals cut a greater percentage of the budget from heritage and cultural programs than from the Department of Defence (Canadian Conference of the Arts Bulletin 1). In Ontario, recent political decisions appear to have been made on the basis of the ascendant paradigm, and even government investment in the cultural industries appears to be eschewed in the race towards reducing not only the deficit but the presence of government in the cultural sphere.

Jeremy Rifkin represents another of the competing voices to the discourse of global competition and increasingly limited responsibility of the state for the well-being of its citizens. In *The End of Work*, he warns that the new information technology combined with the current environment of corporate re-engineering pose a threat of mass unemployment and social unrest (162). Arguing that "the transition into a Third Industrial Revolution throws into question many of our most cherished notions about the meaning and direction of progress," he calls for alternatives to formal work which will engage the energies and talents of future generations faced with structural unemployment and underemployment (217).

Though the most recent figures in both Canada and the U.S. suggest an increase in employment, there is little indication of the nature of those jobs or their long-term impact on employment trends of the future. Moreover, demographics confirm the aging of our population. In the long term, cultural capital, lifelong learning, and the arts will be of critical importance to the creation of what UNESCO has termed a "fully active society" in which the roles of leisure and volunteerism will shift dramatically (World Commission, *Draft Preliminary Outline* 3).

Creativity and imagination will be essential to job creation, higher levels of economic activity, increased exports and increased productivity.[6] To address these issues we need a policy which recognizes the interconnectedness of the cultural portfolio with education and with technology, moving beyond the federal/provincial jurisdictional debates which have precluded comprehensive strategies.

If Canadians outside Quebec are tired of the ongoing debate around constitutional issues and Quebec's place in confederation, the national response to the 1995 October referendum indicates that they are not willingly prepared to abandon the notion of Canada. The question being addressed by every sector and in every discipline is what kind of Canada will we see. With the increasing tensions between globalization and localization, Canada urgently requires a cultural policy framework which can take into account both the spatial and temporal factors which continue to shape our experience as a nation in this shifting world.

Though neoconservatives argue that cultural projects serve only the interests of a particular group in society and that public policy must submit to the requirements of limited government, these responsibilities cannot be abandoned to the private market. The challenge is to clarify common national goals and aspirations, and to determine the public policies required to support them. As we enter the 21st century dominated by discussions of debt and deficit, Canadians, and particularly their political leaders, need to develop a new paradigm which confirms the importance of the arts and culture to the public interest and the critical role of the sector to our future as a nation.

In order to articulate principles for a cultural policy for Canada in the 21st century, it is necessary first to examine, at least briefly, the historic evolution of Canadian cultural policy. I then consider contemporary trends and directions in relation to changing demographics, the new technologies, globalization and the increasing importance of culture in the knowledge era. In this discussion, I identify what I consider to be some of the key issues that must be addressed.

Canadian Culture:
The Historical Case

MODEL 1: *Cultural Identity and National Cultural Policy*

In their comparative research on government policy on the arts Milton Cummings Jr. and Richard Katz identify reasons that bring a state to intervene in the arts and cultural sector (350–368). The political and cultural objectives which they identify might very well have been drawn from a Canadian case study. First among them is the establishment or reinforcement of national identity and the promotion of national unity. Joined to this is a policy of "cultural defence," prompted by the fear of "cultural imperialism" which threatens national sovereignty.

As has been often noted, the English Canadian state predates the development of a Canadian nationality. MacKenzie King, bemoaning the fractured state of Canada, was wont to ask the question that continues to preoccupy us: "Has Canada got an identity — this everlasting, frustrating, humiliating question" (Jones 388). Searching to strengthen a sense of common purpose among Canadians, he established the National Film Board in 1939. Nationhood, national identity and cultural defence have, in fact, been at the heart of Canadian policies in support of cultural development as evidenced by the creation of Canada's major national institutions. In the 1920s, the National Gallery of Canada embarked on an ongoing project to promote Canadian art and through it a sense of national identity throughout the country (see Zemans, "Establishing the Canon"). The CBC, established in 1933 in response to American domination of the airwaves, was described by the Massey-Levesque Commission as Canada's "greatest single agency for national unity." Though the 1968 Broadcasting Act which stipulated that "the national broadcasting service should contribute to the development of national unity and provide for a continuing expression of Canadian identity," was, according to Paul Schafer and Andre Fortier, the first time that a formal link was made between a cultural policy and "national unity" per se (22), national identity and the attempt to create a shared vision of Canada were, in fact, at the heart of the CBC's creation.

Shaped by the compelling vision of nationhood and national identity, the power of symbolic language and the case for nationhood have historically dominated the federal discourse, particularly in the face of a market flooded with American cultural products.[7] These forces continue to dominate the policy discussion, though one must wonder at the naivete of creating a Canadian Flag Day or establishing another committee on national unity rather than addressing the underlying cultural issues central to any solution of Canada's problems.

Herein lies one of the major Canadian policy ironies. Despite arguments that national cultural policies and national institutions are becoming obsolete in a globalized environment, the Liberal party campaigned for office in 1992 on a platform which located culture as a cornerstone of nation building. Recognizing the centrality of Canadian culture to the national project, the Liberal government is currently engaged in a desperate struggle to define the common experience of its citizens.

In fact, Ottawa's current attempt to reduce the role of the state in the cultural sector in favour of markets and private enterprise runs counter to not only our historic recognition of the importance of national strategies but to the government's own understanding of the role of cultural policy as a tool of nationhood. The increasing tensions over the cultural exemption in NAFTA are but one result of this clash of basic premises. Capitulation to the American "free market" mode of regulation (and de-regulation) is undermining not only the centrality of the state but the capacity of the cultural institutions and national policies designed to sustain the Canadian nation.

MODEL 2: *The Democratization of Culture*

Recognizing the broad purpose of cultural policy, the Massey-Levesque Report recommended national strategies, emphasizing the importance of support for the humanities and the social sciences within the post-secondary educational system and for the support of artists and artistic creation across the country. The report contained a litany of examples which illustrated the problems facing the arts in Canada. Artists could not earn a living in Canada. The country relied principally on international touring companies for professional performing arts productions. Few books were published here; Canadian text books were almost all published in the United States. Canadian school children were more familiar with American presidents than with Canadian prime ministers.

Access was key in a sparsely populated country with significant regional disparities and isolation. "Democratization of culture" was at the core of the establishment of the Canada Council; the evolution of its policies saw support for a growing number of arts organizations and individual artists across the country. Infrastructure development, however, was contingent on the participation of provincial and municipal governments and was consequently uneven, a situation that has become increasingly problematic.

At the heart of this approach lay a critical tension between the centre and the regions and between the cities and the hinterland. Touring (particularly by the larger performing arts organizations) and translation, as well as the dissemination of exhibitions, materials and human resources by the national museums and galleries, were intended to increase shared understanding. The development of major or "flagship" organizations, particularly in the performing arts, was a key element in this strategy and these were charged with touring their work to other parts of the country.

That Canadians outside of Ontario and Quebec often perceived such strategies to be elitist and dominated by a central Canadian aesthetic should not be surprising (Litt). Justified on the basis of maximizing limited resources and making artistic "excellence" broadly accessible, the approach was responsible for the establishment and/or growth of most of the major arts organizations and the principal training schools in the country, institutions which remain heavily concentrated in central Canada and regional capitals. Yet it failed to adequately address local needs and initiatives.[8] There remained a strong sense that smaller centres of population were being offered their "legitimate" cultural heritage and that a sparsely populated country should look to a policy of distribution rather than a diffuse base of cultural production and creativity.

MODEL 3: *Cultural Democracy: Watering the Flowers*

If, in the first half century of Canadian cultural policy, nationalism dominated the relationship of culture and the state, the 1970s saw the shaping of a strategy which emphasized the creation "cultural democracy" — a strategy first articulated for the future of Canadian cultural policy by Gerard Pelletier in 1968. In a speech that year Pelletier specified his government's objectives to:

> make available to the masses the means for cultural expression to ensure that as many as possible participate . . . for cultural equalization payments for regions which might be termed cultural deserts . . . for French- and English-speaking minorities . . . for entire zones in our cities which, through low levels of economic activity, are cut off from cultural life because they lack the necessary institutions. (qtd. in Schafer and Fortier 26)

In 1970 Pelletier summarized these objectives as: democratization; decentralization; pluralism; federal-provincial co-operation and international cooperation.

This approach, strongly premised on a series of horizontal movements, required participants at the national level to find the means for *local* cultural expression. Though it was never an either/or situation, the notion of "cultural democracy" (significantly enhanced by growing participation and partnerships at the provincial level) gradually gained priority over the theory of the "democratization of culture," which was, characteristically, vertically integrated from top to bottom and premised on the notion of disseminating "the best a nation has to offer" to the regions and the hinterlands.

In the seventies the strategy of decentralization represented a significant policy shift on the Canadian scene. Echoing similar initiatives in Europe at the time, its thrust likely reflected Canada's participation in the international meetings organized by UNESCO where cultural issues were increasingly framed in terms of participation and "cultural democracy."[9] As increased decentralization became a key policy focus in national cultural institutions, particularly the Canada Council, it also served as a catalyst for increased participation at the provincial and municipal levels, and for private sector support.

Though the objective of federal public funding was, after 1968, often framed in the rhetoric of unity, its implementation became significantly engaged with the empowerment of regional voices. Indeed the distribution of both artists and arts organizations has become considerably less concentrated since the early seventies, as

16

have the patterns of cultural supply and demand, not only in the not-for-profit sector but also in the cultural industries which experienced major growth in regional publishing houses and periodicals as well as in film production. An unwieldy strategy if the bottom line is the only measurement, the approach has been relatively successful in achieving broad national opportunities.

Along with the broadening of the base for creation and support for the growth of the cultural industries, this period witnessed a significant growth in employment and productivity and the creation of indigenous Canadian cultural products in centres across the country. With this growth came a shift in the basis for arts funding. Though there had always been a tacit understanding that culture, like education, health and the environment, is a "public good," and a well-organized, articulate, though small, lobby continued to advocate this view, this rationale became less important in determining public policy. During the 1970s the cultural industries and the growing importance of cultural tourism increasingly supplanted the place of the "public good" as the basis for government support of the sector (Mulcahy and Swaim 55). As evidence of the economic impact of the arts and cultural sector grew, economic justification gained ascendancy in policy creation. The multiplier effect and arguments of cultural economists were increasingly invoked to prove the value of the arts to society. This shift in emphasis has come more and more to supplant the belief that, at the heart of a national policy, must be the capacity of a vibrant cultural domain to serve the public interest, by forging what Schiller called a common or communal sense (Gemeinsinn), concretizing and facilitating the relationship of individual and community central to social life (Schiller 27).

The 1982 report of the Federal Cultural Policy Review Committee (Applebaum-Hebert) attempted to redefine the situation, making the economist's "merit good" case for the arts and particularly for the creative artist in society. Acknowledging that though "a successful cultural policy will achieve desirable economic, social and political results as by-products," the Report argued that "these should not be allowed to dictate the aims or content of cultural policy itself" (8). It placed great emphasis on artistic creativity, over and above any of the other facets of our cultural life, stating that "the role of creative artists should be given special priority in consideration of cultural policies in order that the public might benefit from the results of creative work" (4).

The American cultural policy critic, Edward Arian who holds artists to be "the wellspring of any national culture," believes that Canada has been much more successful than the U.S. in creating a true cultural democracy and he attributes this success directly to the work of the Canada Council (15). He bases his assessment on three criteria: the necessity of artistic experience for individual development, good citizenship and a decent life; the right of all citizens in a democracy to artistic experience and the obligation of the state toward the creative artist; and the belief that people of all classes and backgrounds desire and respond to the opportunity to experience art. This, he suggests, can happen only when they are given the opportunity to define their cultural needs and determine the programs that will best meet those needs and express their individual identities (4).

Though Arian is overly generous in his assessment of our achievements, he is correct in his basic assumption. Due largely to the Canadian commitment to the arm's length tradition and the central role that artists have played in the development of Council policies and indirectly to the broader influence of those policy decisions, Canada has been more successful than almost any other English-speaking nation in supporting individual artists and providing access to the professional arts.

We have, however, failed to find the balance essential to the success of this strategy. While we have been relatively successful in acknowledging the role of the professional artist in society, we have proven less able to provide citizens with the opportunity to experience and participate in the arts, in part because of the structural deformities that handicap our distribution systems and particularly due to our failure to ensure the place of the arts in our educational systems. Thus Canada has yet to develop a true cultural participatory model. While this is clearly a local and provincial responsibility, national policies in countries such as the Netherlands, Sweden, France and Australia have been successful in stimulating development in this field. More often than not, jurisdictional issues in Canada, particularly in education, have precluded the collaboration necessary to develop national strategies, allowing governments to share research and resources. By working in cooperation with the provinces, the potential exists to create a coherent communications, education and arts and cultural policy with responsibility for both communications and content situated in the Department of Canadian Heritage.

The Contemporary Scene

CURRENT ISSUES I: *Demographics*

If cultural democracy has been a central element in the development of national cultural strategies, cultural heterogeneity is at the root of the essential paradox that is Canada. It is both the defining character of the Canadian experience and the reason that Canada is so difficult to define. The contestation of identities in an increasingly diverse country represents an essential challenge to the establishment of any fixed notion of identity and to the conventional notion of unity.

Historically defined by region, language and religion, Canada has never been monocultural. Confederation was a reconciliation between regional and national ambitions, and between Francophone and Anglophone cultures (Spry 179). Bilingualism and biculturalism, native self-government, multiculturalism, and the Charter of Rights and Freedoms represent attempts to manage our diversity and to create "One Canada" out of the competing paradigms.

Respecting the centrality of "local experience," Canada's multicultural policy has provided an ideological construct for accommodating diversity while attempting to sustain legitimacy for individuals as members of groups, and for groups, as well as individuals, as constituent elements of the polity. Though our multicultural policy is admired internationally and considered a model by UNESCO, critics blame the policy for devaluing what it purports to promote, fracturing Canadian society by its insistence on hyphenated Canadians and the creation of "identity communities."[10] While the principle of the "mosaic" has arguably served us better than the U.S. "melting pot," there is no doubt that the policy contains within it, particularly as implemented, the seeds of continual struggle and even discord.

Canadian artists have been among the most vociferous critics of the policy. The implementation of multiculturalism, they claim, created a two-tiered system. Artists have resented their categorization on the bases of race and ethnicity as an element in the multiculturalism portfolio and their exclusion or peripheralization by the major cultural institutions. They argue that there cannot be a policy based on "excellence" for artists and organizations who represent the dominant cultures, and a politically motivated strategy of support for a static model of heritage and indigenous cultures. Challenging the bias in government institutions and agencies, artists are cogent in their argument that mainstream public institutions must support the arts as living and vital elements of human and social experience in both heritage and contemporary practice.

Awareness of the need for a policy premised on true cultural democracy rather than on external difference has (somewhat late in the day) begun to influence cultural policies at every level of the Canadian experience. Still, the unresolved tensions inherent in such diversity undermine any idea of a fixed identity or of fixed relationships between identities. These tensions are exquisitely described in Robert Lepage's remarkable theatrical works, "Tectonic Plates" and "The Seven Streams of the River Ota." As Mexican-born artist and writer, Guillermo Gomez-Pena has said, "the border is the juncture, not the edge" (qtd. in *Our Creative Diversity* 7).

Sociologists John Berry and Jean Laponce, who have analyzed various approaches to ethnicity, understand the impossibility of premising the discussion on simplistic distinctions between assimilation and separatism. They suggest a "new coalition"

allowing identity to be dominated neither by narrow nationalism nor by official culture but . . . created by a multilogue among all those groups that have a contribution to make — redefining membership, ethnicity, culture, and nation through change and creativity. (70)

The challenge now is to build on what we have accomplished, enhancing understanding between communities and providing opportunities for participation, exchange, and collaboration. Our artists and their creations are critical to this process. As the Harvard Committee on Liberal Education pointed out, "the arts are probably the deepest and most powerful of educative forces" in contemporary

Western societies. Richard Gwyn writes "It's our writers of fiction, that ever-lengthening international list from Margaret Atwood and Robertson Davies to Michael Ondaatje, Rohinton Mistry, Alice Munro, Mordecai Richler, Carol Shields and M.G. Vassanji, who express most clearly the Canadian voice" (287). Today one can enumerate such lists in every art form but policies are required to sustain these voices and those of their younger counterparts and to ensure that their voices are heard.

CURRENT ISSUES 2: *Technology*

Nicholas Negroponte is on the road these days, promoting *Being Digital* and his vision of the replacement of the nation state by a technological environment in which "physical space will be irrelevant and time will play a different role" (7). Though Canada is on his itinerary, Canadians, it would appear, do not need much convincing. In its 1994 report, the Special Joint Committee of the Senate and the House of Commons reviewing Canadian foreign policy, observed, "Globalization is erasing time and space, making borders porous, and encouraging continental integration; ... national sovereignty is being reshaped and the power of national governments to control events reduced" (*Report on Foreign Policy* 1).

Robert Babe offers a sobering antidote to Negroponte's enthusiasm for the new technological world, describing what he calls the competing myths of "technological nationalism" and "technological determinism," and the increasing domination of the latter to the detriment of Canadian cultural life. In a recent paper, he traces the growing power of technological determinism in the evolution of communications policy in Canada. In 1929, the Aird Commission transformed the communications environment from a vehicle for American programs into a communication medium that, opposing continentalist cultural pressures, was designed to be "non-commercial, educative and enlightening, Canadian in content and character, and owned and controlled as public enterprise by Canadians to help build community and nationhood." But, Babe argues, since the early 1980s we have reversed the process.

Canada now has one of the most elaborate and sophisticated cable systems in the world, but most of the stories available to us are

American and only about 14% of all the fiction carried on English Canadian television is Canadian (Canada, Mandate Review Committee 22). We've become the best in the world at distributing other people's cultures!

Babe is as definitive as Ursula Franklin about the significance of this shift. He sees "technology," "convergence" and "information revolution" . . . as code words, rhetorically substituting for "global capitalism, transnational enterprise, international market-forces, [and] dominant economic interests." Canadians are being propagandized "into thinking that convergence, the information highway, privatization, and deregulation of communication are necessary and inevitable." Babe warns of the danger of a medium purported to be neutral and universal which is in reality "one of capitalism's most potent propaganda weapons" (27).

Yet, even in Negroponte's new technological world, it will be content, not hardware, which provides the capacity to give meaning to human endeavour and to the ongoing struggle to re/create a nation. In the fall of 1995 the Canadian Conference of the Arts called on the government to ensure that there continues to be a space for the Canadian imagination in the new technological environment ("Claiming a Space"). Within a marketplace increasingly dominated by American popular culture and a distribution system providing largely foreign content, Canada is faced with the enormous challenge of determining how Canadian creation can be developed, shared and marketed. The 1995 report of the Information Highway Task Force insisted that the "new networks must carry content that reflects the distinctiveness of our cultures; . . . it is the content that will allow all citizens to see themselves as full participants in the information society" (xviii, xxi).

Despite predictions that content regulations will be increasingly difficult to enforce, communications lawyer and policy expert Peter Grant thinks a combination of regulation and investment strategies, along with a strong broadcasting mandate, are required to reinforce Canadian content requirements. To address the growing pressure from the U.S., Grant echoes the Canadian Conference of the Arts in urging that Canada partner with those European countries, such as France, which are also defending their ability to create and disseminate their own cultural products. The alternative is the risk of being "pecked to death in negotiations" (16). The focus of new policies, Grant believes, must be support for new Canadian production — content is at the heart of the issue.

Making Our Voices Heard, the recent Juneau report on broadcasting and film policy in Canada which examined the CBC, the NFB and Telefilm, presents a refreshing new (or perhaps old) perspective, eschewing the prevailing myth of technological determinism. Instead it returns to first principles regarding the public interest, articulating the role which public institutions play in the maintenance of civic society. Stressing the importance of an indigenous television and film production industry, it emphasizes the need to blend public and private sector goals. Central to the report is a renewed CBC television (both English and French) with program services that are "distinctly and almost totally Canadian [offering] a clear and intelligent alternative to commercial television [and] committed to quality, innovation and public service" (100). CBC television should maintain an "active local and regional programming role and position itself as a leading content provider in the new and emerging media, much as the corporation did in the early days of radio and television" (102). The report also recommends that the Broadcasting Act should mandate innovative programming which includes "interests and tastes not adequately provided for" and "programming devoted to culture and the arts" (124). Like the Aird Report, *Making our Voices Heard* should be recognized as a wake-up call.

CURRENT ISSUES 3: *Weaving the Warp and the Woof:*
Globalization and the Economic Challenge

In the context of globalization and of fiscal restraint, we must return to basic principles, establishing what the role of government is and what government can do to ensure the viability of our culture. If the function of neoconservatism has been to reduce the public sphere, the issue now is to ensure its survival.

Central to the Juneau task force recommendations is the design and deployment of a National Content Development Strategy which addresses the respective roles of the CBC, Telefilm Canada and the National Film Board in developing Canadian film and video as well as multimedia products. The Information Highway task force concluded that culture is a "fundamental national process; the on-going dialogue focusing a diverse spectrum of perspectives into a shared vision of Canada. Canadians . . . must be able to provide and access their own content on the Information Highway" (121).

Despite the rhetoric of two successive governments and the stock-pile of government-commissioned reports, neither the Mulroney Conservatives nor the current Liberal government have had the will or the vision to implement a coherent federal cultural policy to ensure Canada's ability to "provide and access" Canadian content.[11]

Deficit reduction has occurred in a vacuum. While Free Trade and the possibility of retaliation virtually paralyzed the Mulroney gov-ernment, the Liberals, despite their stated policies, have responded to such external challenges in what can only be described as an inconsistent manner. Caving in on the Ginn/Paramount sale and Viacom takeover, they went the extra distance in the case of *Sports Illustrated.* While continuing to reduce postal subsidies and support to publishing, they held the line on the issue of control in the Borders dispute. After years of budget reductions to the national institutions and program decimation in the support to the cultural sector, the government finally began in the 1996 budget to deal with tax strate-gies, albeit in a limited manner. As direct subsidies are reduced, indirect strategies of support become increasingly important tools in policy implementation. Tax regulations, like the second phase of copyright legislation, to be introduced shortly, are critical elements in the development of a coherent strategy.[12] They must, however, be understood as part of a comprehensive approach involving both direct and indirect support, rather than as solutions in their own right.

Acknowledging that long-term return from investment in artists and the arts is real and substantial and that if it were left to market forces there would be almost no room for Canadian production, the Macdonald Royal Commission on Economic Union and Develop-ment argued for strong public support of this sector, recommending that the "Government of Canada pursue a more aggressive policy of support for indigenous cultural expression as a concomitant of a bilateral trade initiative" (*Summary of Conclusions and Recommen-dations* 13). We have spent the better part of this century developing the institutions that should be central to policy development but we do not have the context in which the necessary planning, coordination and restructuring must take place to accommodate the new environment.

The Juneau report provides a model for addressing cultural policy from a strategic perspective. Encompassing broadcasting, film and video and the new media, it acknowledges the critical balance that is required between centrifugal and centripetal approaches, between software and hardware, and between the public and private sectors. Its recommendations indicate that extensive restructuring is required. The authors are adamant about the central importance of public broadcasting and argue that Telefilm and the National Film Board must adjust their mandates and operations to complement the CBC. Issues of language and cultural diversity, the critical role that the national broadcaster has played in the North and the need for greater regional and local participation are addressed as central to a renewed capacity for "reflect[ing] Canada to Canadians." The report positions the public broadcaster as part of a larger plan which recognizes the centrality of the creator and the importance of copyright legislation and which integrates the public and private sectors to create Canadian programming through a combination of direct funding and tax incentives.

These recommendations would have been received differently had they been perceived as the core of a defined and comprehensive policy. The immediate public and government reactions to the principles advocated in the report were, however, swamped by a negative response to the task force's proposal for an alternative funding structure, the Communications Distribution Tax.[13] Yet consistent funding is critical.

It would be a tragedy if this report were to meet the fate of most of other studies that have recommended a creative rather than a technology-driven or market-driven response to cultural policy issues. All reports and recommendations to the contrary, the rhetoric of national unity is hollow. Unity is not a strategy in itself; it may however be the by-product of a clearly coordinated approach which gives voice to the diversity of Canadian experience.

Conclusion

A renewed cultural policy must acknowledge the importance of both contemporary artistic creation and heritage in shaping national vision and capacity, supporting creation and its production and dissemination in the arts, of ensuring sustainable cultural industries and of the individual citizen's right to access to and participation in arts and cultural activities. The artist and artistic creation must be central. Such a policy must cut across issues of centre and region, urban and hinterland, language and ethnicity.

A coherent cultural policy will be premised on an understanding of the importance of the artist's role and of cultural expression to national well-being. Commitment to adequate and stable federal government support of our public institutions is critical. At the same time, we must develop new models to encourage and build private support for the cultural sector.

Important not only in the development of a national consciousness, as the Juneau task force reiterated, public institutions have a role to play in interpreting Canada and Canadians to the rest of the world. The writings of Margaret Atwood, Robertson Davies and Lucy Maud Montgomery are among our most successful exports. Like Radio Canada International, they have the capacity to shape the understanding of Canada in the imaginations of people around the world. The British Council, the Alliance Francaise, the Goethe Institute, the Japan Foundation and United States Information Agency offer evidence of the importance other countries have attached to the export of their cultures and the development of their images abroad. Today the Canadian Department of Foreign Affairs pays lip-service to the notion of culture as the third pillar of foreign policy; yet only five years ago External Affairs was prepared to abandon its capacity to act in this field which it deemed extraneous to the Department's central mission.

While other countries have defined the arts and culture as "cultural ambassadors," principal tools in positioning their countries internationally, often through dedicated programs, Canada has had an uneven history of recognizing this sector's importance in foreign relations or in projecting its image abroad. Lip service will not suffice.

The Department of Foreign Affairs and International Trade must restructure its operations and its allocation of resources, integrating the active promotion of the arts and cultural industries into its foreign policy objectives. But it cannot act unilaterally. A true working partnership is required between federal cultural institutions and the Department with collaboration and planning that involves trade commissioners as well as cultural representatives. Reciprocity must also be high on the agenda; cultural diplomacy is not only about promoting our artists and products abroad but involves an exchange of ideas, a fact which Canada has too often ignored.

The shadow of globalization looms large over Canadian policy-makers. Despite the cultural exemption obtained in the FTA and NAFTA, policy in the cultural sector is shaped (if that is not to strong a word for current activity) defensively, with a fearful glance towards our neighbours to the south and the knowledge of impending retribution. Canada must determine what strategies best serve its interests in international trade negotiations. Will exemption or regulation in the cultural sector better protect our arts and cultural industries and allow us to undertake new initiatives as they are required? The research remains to be done. We must create strategic alliances with other countries facing the same dilemma. Despite the fact that, in the past, other countries have looked to Canada for models; cultural sovereignty is not a uniquely "Canadian" problem.

Central to any future policy is the imperative to reunite the culture and communications portfolios. The decision to separate these responsibilities was made by a former government which appeared bent on pacifying the Americans. The current government was elected on a platform which opposed this strategy. To deal effectively with the issues, it must make culture central to its agenda and understand that the issues concerning hardware and software cannot be seen in isolation. Indeed, our greatest problem appears to be the inability to consider the cultural domain as a whole and to develop strategies that encompass both content and technology.

In the past we have argued that constitutional issues preclude national strategies; but there is no impediment to partnerships amongst all levels of government. National strategies are required to complement local and provincial initiatives. What we lack is the vision to see the issues holistically. In *Blood and Belonging*, Michael

Ignatieff describes the struggle between the civic and the ethnic nation, between those "who still believe that a nation should be home to all, and that race, colour, religion and creed should be no bar to belonging, and those who want their nation to be home only to their own." The civic nation has been the defining vision upon which Canada has been built, one in which culture remains an evolving concept and the definition of identity, the site of ongoing contestation.

Canadian citizens will continue to identify with the local while becoming increasingly at home in the international sphere. But we also require a central public space, not for the imposition of any single meta-narrative but for the provision of real sharing and exchange — a space for the Canadian imagination. The balance is precarious. Should the dispersed spaces lose sight of the centre, the centre could collapse.

NOTES

[1] The current trade surplus in cultural services and products enjoyed by the U.S. in Canada defines the historic problem. The Canadian Conference of the Arts cited the 1991 figure as 4.4 billion; the exports of goods and services in arts and cultural industries totalled 1.5 billion and imports were 5.9 billion ("Building the Creative Infrastructure," 9).

[2] In 1987 *Vital Links* reported that 76% of books sold in Canada were imported; 97% of theatrical screen time went to imported films, 89% of earnings in the sound-recording industry accrued to 12 foreign-controlled firms that principally marketed imported popular music, and over 90% of dramatic television presentations were non-Canadian in origin. As the document points out, "the concern is not with the ease of access to the products of other cultures. It is rather with the difficulty of access to our own products, a difficulty that is primarily a function of the economics of the cultural industries, which place the cheaper, mass-marketed, imported products at such a distinct advantage . . ." (11)

[3] See J. Zemans, "And the Lion Shall Lie Down with the Lamb" and Fagan (A2). The notwithstanding clause gives the U.S. the right to assess the equivalent commercial impact of any new cultural policies adopted by Canada and impose a countervail against any part of the Canadian economy. The structure of the clause does not leave Canada any channel of appeal for the assessed damages to American interests or input as to where they apply the punitive measures. In the case of the split-run editions, the U.S. plans to take Canada to the World Trade Organization

28

and to challenge the basic argument of cultural sovereignty particularly in the area of the cultural industries.

[4] "Short wave radio service supposed to go off air April 1, 1996," *The Globe*, January 18. "CBC report links culture to national unity." C1.

[5] The Report stated (Canada, Royal Commission on National Development in the Arts, 274): "If we, as a nation, are concerned with the problem of defence, what we may ask ourselves, are we defending? We are defending civilization, our share of it, our contribution to it. The things with which an inquiry deals are the elements which give a civilization its character and its meaning. It would be paradoxical to defend something which we are unwilling to strengthen and enrich, and which we even allow to decline."

[6] The arts and cultural labour force has grown by 190,000 since 1971 or 122% (total labour force growth was 58%); has created 360,000 direct jobs and 137,000 indirect jobs in the sector (growing from 1.8% of labour force to 2.5%); and has contributed $22 billion to the national economy (3.7 % of Canada's gross domestic product in 1990–91). The federal treasury receives more than $650 million in taxes from cultural industries. The cost of a job created in these industries is approximately $10,000 compared to $100,000 in light industry and $200,000 in heavy industry (Canadian Conference of the Arts, "Putting Creativity and Imagination to Work" 1–2).

[7] *The Ties that Bind* (Parliament, House of Commons, Standing Committee), the 1992 report by an all-party committee, reaffirms the critical role of the arts and cultural sector in the experience of nationhood.

[8] Susan Crean has argued that Canada Council supported large organizations which represented "Official Culture," monopolized state funds and turned the rest of Canada's creative people into guerilla warriors (268). Bernard Ostry contests this argument (113, 131, 194 for example).

[9] In 1979 Gerard Pelletier headed the Canadian delegation to the historic Venice Intergovernmental Conference organized by UNESCO which examined the institutional, administrative and financial aspects of cultural policy (Schafer and Fortier 31). UNESCO remained the only forum in which a thorough and longitudinal analysis of cultural policy and its impact were undertaken in the sixties and seventies.

[10] To make this case, Gwyn (198–99) quotes Neil Bissoondath who argues that "Our approach to multiculturalism encourages the devaluation of what it claims to protect and promote. Culture becomes an object for display rather than the heart and soul of the individual formed by it" (244).

[11] While the myriad reports of past task forces, royal commissions and parliamentary committees are an unmined resource, their recommendations have for the most part been ignored. In the arts sector, for example, recommendations in the Applebaum/Hebert report on federal cultural policy (1982), and the Bovey report (1986), or the White/Rossignol task force on training in the arts (1992), among others, remain relevant today, despite the shifting environment.

[12] Revisions to tax policies have been recommended by both the Canada Council and the cultural industries. To compensate for underfunding, *A Time for Action*, the report on the future of the music industry stressed the importance of specific tax strategies as incentives for investment and alternatives to direct government funding (Rensetti C9). Echoing the House of Commons Committee's 1992 identification of revised tax policies for support of the not-for-profit sector as key to the survival

of Canadian arts organizations, the Canada Council has proposed a number of revisions to current tax policies. The recent 1996 budget adopted two of the Council's recommendations, exempting donations of property which has appreciated in value from capital gains tax and raising the limit of charitable donations from 20% to 50% of income.
[13] The immediate public (and government) reaction to the report was negative and directed almost entirely at the task force's proposal for an alternative funding structure — the Communications Distribution Tax. The 7.5% tax on communication distribution services was intended to fully fund the CBC and was proposed along with an extra percentage point to replace capital appropriations. Concurrent with the implementation of this tax, the report proposed that RDI's and Newsworld's minimal subscriber fees be eliminated. Since businesses can recover the GST on their "inputs," their effective rate of tax would be 7.5% less. (It is interesting to note that Rifkin proposes a value-added tax on all computer, information and telecommunications products and services (271).

WORKS CITED

Adorno, Theodor. *The Culture Industry: Selected Essays on Mass Culture.* Ed. J.M. Bernstein. London: Routledge, 1991.

Arian, Edward. *The Unfulfilled Promise: Public Subsidy of the Arts in America.* Philadelphia: Temple University Press, 1989.

Audley, Paul. "Cultural Industries Policy: Objectives, Formulation and Evaluation." *Canadian Journal of Communication* 19 (1994).

Babe, Robert E. "Media Technology and the Great Transformation of Canadian Cultural Policy." (Conference on Media Policy, National Identity and Citizenry in Changing Democratic Societies: The Case of Canada; Canadian Studies Center, Duke University, Durham, NC, 6–7 Oct. 1995.) Typescript, University of Ottawa, Aug. 1995.

Berry, John, and Jean Laponce, eds. *Ethnicity and Culture in Canada.* Toronto: University of Toronto Press, 1995.

Blacking, John. "Culture and the Arts." Washington, National Endowment for the Arts, 1986.

Canada. Department of Communications. *Vital Links: Canadian Cultural Industries.* [Ottawa]: Minister of Supply and Services, 1987.

——. Information Highway Advisory Council. *Connection, Community, Content: The Challenge of the Information Highway.* Ottawa: Minister of Supply and Services, 1995.

——. Federal Cultural Policy Review Committee. *Report of the Federal Cultural Policy Review Committee,* Ottawa, Minister of Supply and Services, 1982.

——. Mandate Review Committee, CBC, NFB, Telefilm. *Making Our Voices Heard:*

Canadian Broadcasting and Film for the 21st Century. Ottawa: Ministry of Supply and Services, 1996.

———. Parliament. House of Commons. Standing Committee on Communication and Culture. *Culture and Communications: The Ties That Bind*. Ottawa: Minister of Supply and Services, 1992.

———. Royal Commission on the Economic Union and Development Prospects for Canada, *Report of the Royal Commission on the Economic Union and Development Prospects for Canada*, Ottawa: Minister of Supply and Services, 1985.

Royal Commission on National Development in the Arts, Letters and Sciences. *Report of the Royal Commission on Development in the Arts, Letters and Sciences, 1949–51*. Ottawa: King's Printer, 1951.

———. *Summary of Conclusions and Recommendations, Royal Commission on the Economic Union and Development Prospects for Canada*, Ottawa: Minister of Supply and Services, 1985.

———. *Report of the Special Joint Committee on Foreign Policy*, Ottawa: Minister of Supply and Services, 1994.

Canadian Conference of the Arts. Bulletin, 03/06/96.

———. Bulletin, 01/10/96.

———. "The Canadian Cultural Sector: Building the Creative Infrastructure." Ottawa, Jan. 1994.

———. "The Canadian Cultural Sector: Putting Creativity and Imagination to Work." Ottawa, 1994.

———. "Claiming a Space for the Canadian Imagination." Ottawa, Fall 1995.

Council of Europe. "Cultural Policy Dossier." News Report No. 1–2/88, ISSN: 0252-0859.

Crean, Susan. *Who's Afraid of Canadian Culture?* Don Mills: General Publishing, 1976.

Cummings, Milton J., Jr., and Richard S. Katz, eds. *The Patron State: Government and the Arts in Europe, North America and Japan*. Oxford: Oxford University Press, 1987.

Dewey, John. *Freedom and Culture*. Buffalo: Prometheus, 1989.

DiMaggio, Paul, and Michael Useem. "Social Class and Arts Consumption: The Origins and Consequences of Class Differences in Exposure to the Arts in America." *Theory and Society* 5.2 (1978).

Fagan, Drew. "Canada to Stand Firm on Cultural Protection." *Globe and Mail* 12 Mar. 1996: A2.

Franklin, Ursula. "Peace, Technology and the Role of Ordinary People." Lois and John Dove Memorial Lecture, University of Toronto, 1995.

Frye, Northrop. *The Modern Century*. Toronto: Oxford University Press, 1967.

Galbraith, John Kenneth. *Economics and the Public Service*. Boston: Houghton Mifflin, 1973.

Grant, Peter. "Will Cable Competitors Support or Threaten Canadian Content?" Transcript, Robarts Seminar, York University, 28 Nov. 1995.

Gwyn, Richard. *Nationalism without Walls: The Unbearable Lightness of Being Canadian*. Toronto: McClelland and Stewart, 1995.

Ignatieff, Michael. *Blood and Belonging: Journeys into the New Nationalism*. London: BBC Books, 1993.

Jones, D.B. *Movies and Memoranda: An Interpretive History of the NFB*. Ottawa: Canadian Film Institute, 1981.

Litt, Paul. "The Massey Commission, Americanization and Canadian Cultural Nationalism." *Queen's Quarterly* 98.2 (1992): 375–87.

Meisel, John. "Flora and Fauna on the Rideau: The Making of Cultural Policy. *How Ottawa Spends: 1988–89*. Ed. Katherine A. Graham. Ottawa: Carleton University Press, 1988.

Mulcahy, Kevin, and Richard Swaim. *Public Policy and the Arts*. Boulder, CO: Westview Press, 1982.

Negroponte, Nicholas. *Being Digital*. New York: Knopf, 1996.

Ostry, Bernard. *The Cultural Connection*. Toronto: McClelland & Stewart, 1978.

Reich, Robert. *The Work of Nations: Preparing Ourselves for 21st Century Capitalism*. New York: Random House, 1992.

Rensetti, Elizabeth. "Recording Industry Underfunded Needs Tax Credit, Study Says." *Globe and Mail* 9 Mar. 1996: C9.

Rifkin, Jeremy. *The End of Work*. New York: Putnam, 1996.

Saul, John Ralston. Position Paper on Culture and Foreign Policy, Prepared for the Special Joint Committee of the House of Commons and the Senate Reviewing Foreign Policy. Typescript, 30 Aug. 1994.

——. *The Unconscious Civilization*. Toronto: Anansi, 1995.

Schafer, D. Paul, and Andre Fortier. *Review of the Federal Policies for the Arts in Canada 1944–1988*. Ottawa: Canadian Conference of the Arts, 1988.

Schiller, Friedrich. *On the Aesthetic Education of Man*. Trans. & Eds. Elizabeth Wilson and L.A. Willoughby. Oxford: Clarendon Press, 1967.

Spry, Irene. "Canadian Culture: Past and Future." *The Strategy of Canadian Culture in the 21st Century*. Ed. Ian Parker, John Hutcheson, and Pat Crawley. Toronto: TopCat Communications, 1988.

Steiner, George. *In Bluebeard's Castle: Some Notes Towards the Re-definition of Culture*. London: Faber and Faber, 1971.

Taylor, Charles. "Atomism." *Philosophical Papers*. Vol. 2. Cambridge: Cambridge University Press, 1985. 187–210.

World Commission on Culture and Development. *Draft Preliminary Outline of the World Report on Culture and Development*. Typescript, San Jose, Costa Rica, Feb. 1994.

——. *Our Creative Diversity: Report of the UNESCO-UN World Commission on Culture and Development*. [Paris]: UNESCO, 1995.

Zemans, Joyce. "And the Lion Shall Lie Down with the Lamb." *American Review of Canadian Studies* (Winter 1994): 509–38.

——. "Establishing the Canon: The Early History of Reproductions at the National Gallery of Canada." *Journal of Canadian Art History* (summer 1995): 6–35.